PORTRAIT OF
IOWA

Introduction by
PAUL ENGLE

Photographs by
JOHN M. ZIELINSKI
and Others

ADAMS PRESS
Minneapolis

Acknowledgement

John M. Zielinski acknowledges the assistance of several Iowa
chambers of commerce and special appreciation to the Iowa Development
Commission (IDC)—in particular, Philip Morgan and Judi Pierick.
And, to the people of Iowa who have so generously allowed him
to photograph them over the last ten years.

Published by
THE ADAMS PRESS
59 Seymour Avenue Southeast
Minneapolis, Minnesota 55414

Captions by John M. Zielinski.
Designed by John M. Zielinski and the Adams Press.
Printed in the United States of America.

Typesetting by Graph-Tronics, Inc. Color separations by Colorbrite, Inc.
Binding by Midwest Editions, Inc. All other manufacturing by Kolorpress,
Inc. Map by Cartography Laboratory, University of Minnesota.

Library of Congress Cataloging in Publication Data

Zielinski, John M.
    Portrait of Iowa.

    1. Iowa—Description and travel—1951-   —Views.
I. Title.
F622.Z53   917.77'03'30222   74-17265
ISBN 0-914828-01-0

CONTENTS

Photograph by John Bean.

Sioux City — once a part of the Sioux Indian nation — is today Iowa's largest northwestern city, with a population of over 100,000. A new highway system, five railroads, and the Missouri River (now open to heavy barge traffic) make it an industrial and transportation center. (Sioux City CofC photograph.)

Ruan Center, Des Moines. The skyline of Iowa's capital and largest city is being drastically altered by new skyscrapers. The Ruan Center is the tallest, with 36 stories.

11

Assembly line of Collins Radio Company in Cedar Rapids — which bears a striking similarity to Iowa cornfields. Collins has provided communications equipment for a number of dramatic uses, including Admiral Byrd's journey to the South Pole, the Apollo flights, and the manned moon explorations. (Collins Radio photograph.)

The twenty-one-story Iowa Electric Tower is one of Cedar Rapids' tallest buildings. The Cedar Rapids skyline is no longer dominated by the massive grain silos of Quaker Oats.

Introduction

by PAUL ENGLE

The tallest point in Iowa is a hog lot on the Sterler family farm near Sibley, Osceola County, in the extreme northwest corner of the state. It could not be more appropriately located.

Look at the map of Iowa and squint a little—there is the stylized outline of a hog, with the snout pushing east between Dubuque and Davenport, an eye at Waterloo, and the beginning of a trotter at Keokuk, the Mississippi River forming the front contour of the hog. The rear of the animal is made by the Missouri River (whose silt-dark water is really hog-colored) from Nebraska City to Sioux City, where the outline continues north to the Minnesota line along the Big Sioux River. There is a squirming, bending line of the Missouri River right west of Sioux City like a pig tail. (Of course, this puts Sioux City in an interesting position!) The state's outline has the chunky, solid, rectangular shape, on the map, of a well-cleaned carcass.

That appearance could not be more appropriate, for Iowa has almost a quarter of all the hogs in the United States. Every year twenty million go to market. Standing downwind on a hot day from that many hogs can give you a sense of the richness of animal life and the glory of the human nose.

Nothing, however, could be more misguided than to think of Iowa as a state happily languishing in the rural nineteenth century while the rest of the country prepares to enter the twenty-first century. Not even with hogs has it remained old-fashioned. Iowa State University at Ames, one of the leading institutions for agriculture in the world, has developed an ultrasonic probe to determine depth of backfat on a hog, one way to find out the quality of the meat beneath that tough, bristly skin. The machine is put over an animal, very short sound waves are beamed into its body. They penetrate the fat layer, but bounce back from the red meat or bone, giving a clear image on a screen of the precise thickness of the fat, which could formerly be done only by killing the creature. This is no longer the overweight, loaded-with-lard porker of years ago, but a scientifically bred and fed length of lean meat. That flowing back line and that beautifully rounded rump are as hand-carved as if done in stone.

Iowa is probing not only the inner space of animals, but the outer space of the universe. When the first American satellite went into orbit, it carried instruments designed and built in the Physics Department at the University of Iowa in Iowa City by Dr. James Van Allen and two Iowa students. Today that same office is receiving information from its equipment on board Pioneer 10 as it comes as close as possible to the magnetic field around the planet Jupiter. The only American ever to win the world-famous Wieniawski violin prize in Poland was Charles Treger, who did so while on the faculty at the University of Iowa. When the C. Y. Stephens Auditorium, with its superb design and its dramatic stage curtain, was opened for its first concert at Iowa State University, the New York Philharmonic played. When the voices of the first astronauts were heard speaking from the moon, it was communication equipment made in Cedar Rapids, Iowa, by Collins Radio Company, which brought those human sounds from that inhuman landscape. The importance of these events is not confined to the state or nation, but is worldwide.

It is not only space, but time, which dramatizes Iowa: In open prairie landscape, in its wooded valleys along its many streams, its quiet small towns, its belief in hard work and in decency to your neighbor, its pure air (which can still burn you in summer and blast you in winter), its willingness to be taxed for top-level education, its cheerful conviction (in spite of some evidence to the contrary) that work and honesty will always produce the good life, Iowa keeps the good qualities of the nineteenth century. In excellence of its industries, which are, of course, related to its convictions about existence, it belongs to the twentieth century: Maytag Washing Machine Company (to express its belief in cleanliness), Amana Refrigeration (the preservation of food is a necessity and a pleasure), Quaker Oats (which shoots wheat out of cannons to puff it and feeds pets as well as people). In its probes into space beyond the comprehension of man, looking for other inhabited planets or hints about the origin of life itself, in its aesthetic originality ("The Nazi Drawings" of Mauricio Lasansky at the University of Iowa, the new wing of the Art Center in Des Moines), in the bold new designs of machinery by John Deere Company, from the humble manure spreader to the majestic combine, Iowa is learning the first tentative steps into the twenty-first century.

To prove that it is really the heart of the heartland, the middle ground between the extremes of American life, Iowa is exactly twenty-fifth in size among the fifty states. With an average of fifty persons per square mile, and a total of 2,800,000 people, Iowa is also twenty-fifth among the states in population. This marvelous balance expresses itself also in the Iowa character, an extremity of moderation. The Great Seal of the State of Iowa is topped by an eagle; from its beak flutters a banner with the bold assertion, "Our Liberties We Prize and Our Rights We Will Maintain." Beneath is an armed soldier to prove that the determination to maintain those rights is absolute. Behind the soldier is a plow, and he looks eager indeed to drop his musket and start turning over a straight furrow. On his right is a large rake and behind that a field of grain. On his left a steamboat paddles up a broad river, a factory chimney modestly pollutes the air, and a schoolhouse quietly waits for its children. In 1846, when Iowa became a state, the Seal was a prophecy of all the interests which would flourish from the first day of statehood to the present, in that same superb balance which made Iowa the precise center of the United States in land area and in population. It is that quality of the strong middle which distinguishes Iowa from the other Midwestern states, identical as they might appear on a map.

Iowa is the weather center for the midmost part of the Midwest. Blizzards blowing out of the Rocky Mountains meet north winds coming down from Canada, which push against softer air blowing up from the Gulf of Mexico, which bump into wet and wild winds running out of the Great Lakes. The first result is a constant turbulence of climate, always unpredictable, always changing, the temperature rising and falling day after day, night after night, rain turning to ice turning to snow. The busiest instrument in the state is the thermometer, whose red column must lead a frantic life as it ranges, in a single day, from deep snow to melting sun in an hour. On November 11th one year the temperature at Ames fell from 65 degrees Fahrenheit to zero in about six hours. This was the great Armistice Day Freeze, killing hogs, cattle, sheep, and turkeys. All of this means that the Iowan lives not "under the weather," but

Gitchie Manitou State Preserve at the very tip of Northwestern Iowa in the Big Sioux River valley. Its name derives from the Indian for "Great Spirit" and legend says it was here that Sitting Bull and other Sioux chiefs gathered to plan the Battle of the Little Big Horn. This 153-acre park is one of eighty state parks, almost all of which are laid out around rivers, streams, or lakes. (IDC photograph.)

Preceding page: View of the Mississippi from the bluff above McGregor. This is the Iowa that explorers Louis Joliet and Father Jacques Marquette first saw when they paddled out of the Wisconsin River and began the exploration of the Mississippi. Today the last of Iowa's commercial fishermen can be found here, competing with ever-increasing barge traffic and a proliferation of houseboats and other pleasure craft. (IDC photograph.)

under all weathers. Such instability of atmosphere produces a stable character (if residents of the state responded rapidly to all shifts in the climate, their personalities would disintegrate — the psychiatrists would be moving in with the patients at mental institutions). Treacherous ice, scalding sun, August days when the humid and oppressive air never moves, February days when the icy wind blows through clothing and the walls of houses at twenty below zero, April days when not only the grass and trees grow but the very air itself seems fertile, October days when the air is crisp as a dried cornhusk and seems stained with the red of leaves — such days make the balanced, middle-way, solid character of Iowa people. Out of suffering, composure.

In between a range of temperatures from thirty below zero to one hundred and ten above, lives a very cool citizen, undismayed even by the risk of tornadoes. Out of the quiet sky suddenly looms a black funnel with wreckage twisting in it (usually only the briefest warning is possible); where it touches the ground, all is destroyed, buildings, animals, men, women, children. During a tornado on my grandfather's farm near Eagle Grove, a straw was driven into the plank of a barn. There have been whole towns all but wiped out on what had been a peaceful summer day. Tornadoes come because cold air out of the north and northwest strikes warm, moist air pushing up from the Gulf. The two fronts wrestle in the sky until their mingled energies writhe together in a descending spiral. Charles City and Oelwein suffered tornadoes on May 15, 1968, with seventeen persons killed, five hundred and thirty injured, and about 53.3 million dollars in damage over the area. Such violence produces tranquillity, in the contradictory Iowa manner, among the people who endure it.

This may be the reason for the extraordinary peacefulness of Iowa's history. Unlike the surrounding states, it had no real hostilities on its soil: a skirmish between white men and red near Des Moines (before it existed), a massacre at Spirit Lake in northwestern Iowa by Sioux, which was not a fight, one cannon ball fired across the Missouri during the Civil War, which harmed no one and lodged in a house. Even when Chief Black Hawk decided to take his warriors against the militia which had occupied his old grounds, he left Iowa (to which he had moved under pressure) and in 1832 crossed the Mississippi into Illinois along the Rock River

Overleaf: Mesquakie Indian boy at the Pow Wow held on the Indian settlement near Tama each August.

Following: Old Order Amish child after Sunday school services, Washington County, near Kalona.

to do his fighting, ending with a bloody defeat at Bad Axe, Wisconsin. Even "Buffalo Bill" (William Cody), born at Le Claire, on the Mississippi River north of Davenport, left his birthplace and went west to slaughter Indians and buffalo with a wonderful equality— if they were there, he shot them. But never in Iowa!

When John Brown trained his few idealistic Quakers of the nonviolent persuasion near West Branch, east of Iowa City, in handling the arms with which he tried to take over Harper's Ferry, the only act of violence committed by one of his men was hugging girls, for which he was censured.

When Inkpadutah, old leader of the Sioux Indians, massacred thirty-two men, women, and children at Spirit Lake, he realized that this was essentially peaceful land and fled west. Later, he saw the approach of General George Custer's cavalry near the Little Big Horn and gave the most crucial alarm in western history. But he left Iowa.

My maternal grandfather, Jacob Reinheimer, peaceful farmer outside Marion, Iowa, rode with the Fifth Iowa Cavalry across Dakota Territory in the Civil War, trying to commit uncivil acts against the Sioux. He never found them, save that one evening, while the big iron pot of beans was bubbling over a fire, figures were seen skulking in the dark. An order was given to tip the kettle into the fire. No shot was fired, but the Battle of Burnt Beans was my grandfather's most violent act. An old man, white of hair and beard, he was proud of a photograph of himself in uniform, pistols in belt, carbine in hand, and beaded moccasins on his feet.

It was typical of Iowa that in the early days when roads did not exist a man was hired to plow a single furrow from Dubuque through Iowa City and on south. He used a sodbreaking plow with a long oak beam, to hold the cutting edge in the rich prairie soil against the resistance of the deep grass roots, and ten oxen. The image of that solitary individual, creeping through that wide and wild landscape, the grass unbroken before him but slashed with a black snake of dirt behind him, the sky immense overhead, the air silent save for the sound of the plow ripping through roots, is the clear symbol of Iowa. The only other sound must have been the man's voice yelling at the oxen. Ironically, it was called the Military Road, as it marked the route for dragoons and foot soldiers, but, typical of the Iowa scene, it was never used in war.

The fundamental rock beneath Iowa is a limestone formed on an ancient ocean bottom. Some of it is the same hard formation found at Niagara Falls, some of it is full of fossils, trilobites, those little early creatures with serrated bodies, and slender shells with delicate winglike tips *(Spirifer pennatus)*. Today limestone is ground and scattered over fields to sweeten the soil. The shape of this inland state was made by water: first, a great sea out of which the limestone beds were dissolved, and then the great ice glaciers coming repeatedly out of the north, grinding up the rocks they carried, ending in Iowa so that this area received the fine dirt and Minnesota received the boulders, gravel, and lakes. It is characteristic of the Iowa luck that even the relentless glaciers, coming out of Canada, gave the state fertility and the surface soil which is so productive. Here and there in pastures and cornfields today you can see a massive granite boulder dropped by the glaciers; I used to slide as a boy on a big one in Bever Park at Cedar Rapids, not knowing it had probably traveled from the Laurentian granite of southern Canada, scraping long lines on its side as it tumbled and rolled south. There are some igneous outcroppings in northeastern Iowa and some Carboniferous beds in the southwest bearing a high-sulphur-content coal, with sandstones here and there, but essentially Iowa people walk and work on the floor of an ocean.

One of the most interesting soils is called loess, a fine-grained brown clay blown by winds out of the states to the northwest of Iowa, capping many hills, overlying the darker loam. In it are tiny, rare fossils called *loesspueppchen,* meaning the little dolls of the dirt. (This soil was dissolved out of the air, loess deriving from the German word to dissolve, just as the limestone was dissolved out of the water — it is obvious that the destiny of Iowa began to be shaped from processes that began uncountable centuries ago. Even ancient geological processes were fortunate!)

There is a saying that the Missouri River is too thick to drink, too thin to plow. That is the look of Iowa's streams, for it is a state of endless small creeks and minor rivers: Raccoon, Wolf, Catfish, Cedar, Nishnabotna, Skunk, Squaw, Mosquito, Turkey, Little Sioux, Upper Iowa, Five Barrel Creek (where dragoons, in a fit of good fortune, once found barrels of whiskey buried along the bank). Just as there are no really huge cities in Iowa, there are no really big rivers, but everywhere the little drainage creeks flow through the

Overleaf: The covered bridge referred to as Cutler or Donahue was built in 1870 and is one of the seven remaining of Madison County's sixteen covered bridges. On the centennial of its construction, the bridge was moved to the Winterset City Park and restored. (Clee Crawford photograph.)

23

LOW·CLEARANCE

11' 4 IN

IMES·BRIDGE·BUILT·AT·WILKINS·MILL·1870

MOVED·TO·CLANTON·1887

fields toward the modest rivers, which flow through low hills with timber on them. The Tête de Mort in northeastern Iowa commemorates an Indian fight in which the Sac destroyed a band of Dakotas, who were thrown (or jumped) from a high cliff. From the air, you can follow the course of the streams, for they are all outlined by small bands of trees, while the open fields run away in all directions, the spring corn looking like tufts on an old-fashioned quilt.

The most typical Iowa creature in its streams is the catfish, an ancient survivor with a skin, not scales, spines which can stab your hand, a wide flat head. It is earth-colored, invisible under the earth-colored water, yet inside it has a sweet, white flesh free of bones which can be cooked and eaten in large chunks. The Chinese regard the catfish from their immense rivers as a great delicacy, and so do the Iowa people who fish for it, knowing that its meat will not have a "fishy" taste. Like carp, the other common fish swimming at the bottoms of Iowa streams (full of dissolved dirt, like the old limestone and the loess soils), catfish are scavengers, eating organic matter like garbage. They are caught by their sense of smell, swimming toward the baits cunningly blended of such appetizing materials as chicken guts or stinking cheese rolled into bread dough. Determined fishermen make their own baits, often burying the mess under manure piles in the sun so that it will ripen and catfish can smell it far away downstream. Secret formulas are treasured like family recipes and passed on from father to son.

The most successful catcher of catfish I ever knew was a woman whose husband worked in a limestone quarry on the banks of the Wapsipinicon River at Stone City, that tiny and beautiful place near Anamosa in eastern Iowa. The narrow road she walked to the river was crushed limestone from her husband's quarry. Days after she had mixed a batch of bait you could smell it on her hands. After fishing, she would can the flesh for winter eating; the fish her husband ate in January had been caught in June from waters he could see as he blasted rock. They also raised vegetables in a large garden along a tiny creek which flowed into the Wapsipinicon River. She canned the vegetables, corn, cabbage, beans, beets. Rows of the zinnias, gladiolis, chrysanthemums, nasturtiums, marigolds ringed the garden with live color. Yet seeing their clothes, their house, so small you had to whisper when you talked in it or your voice would

26

Palisades-Kepler State Park on the Cedar River four miles west of Mount Vernon. Known for its huge limestone cliffs, the park is an example of the outcroppings of limestone to be found along most Iowa rivers. The stone provided a cheap and accessible building material for early settlers. (IDC photograph.)

Zuber's Restaurant, Homestead. The town is part of the Amana Colonies, known for their homestyle dinners. Founded as a communal colony in 1855, Amana became a corporation in 1932. Otto Zuber, at the end of the table, was the first employee hired by Amana Refrigeration and here celebrates his retirement after forty years.

Basilica of St. Francis Xavier, Dyersville. (IDC photograph.)

be too loud, their battered forks and dishes, some city people would have regarded them as poor. In a state of rich resources, they were rich in everything but money. They ate better than the rich of many countries. They were cheerful. They made a life.

Food is of course a serious matter in Iowa, as it dominates the life of the state and feeds the hungry of the world. If you visit a family on the farm or in a small town, you must eat as well as talk, no matter what time of day. Food is a presence in Iowa homes. You are introduced to it as if it were another person.

The world's greatest shortage is protein, the substance Iowa produces in greatest abundance. If one phrase could be added to the motto on the Great Seal of the state it might be: "Our Liberties We Prize and Our Rights We Will Maintain — and We Will Raise the Damndest Amount of Protein You Ever Saw." Much of the world consumes grain as grain directly — wheat, rice — but Iowa also converts grain into protein-rich meat (a wasteful if delicious product).

Barges from loading docks along the Missouri and Mississippi rivers (Iowa is the only state bounded east and west by navigable rivers) carry corn, soybeans, wheat to New Orleans, for transshipment to Asia and Europe. The farmer who once saw his market as the local elevator, as Omaha, Chicago, Kansas City, now thinks of Copenhagen (soybean cakes for cattle producing milk to make into cheese to sell back to Iowa!), Tokyo (where soybeans become *tofu*, bean curd, in a thousand dishes), the Soviet Union buying wheat and corn, or mainland China. His grandfather may have regarded himself as strictly a citizen of Iowa, with Washington a very distant and suspect city, but now the Iowa farmer takes policy and advice from Washington (not always happily) and knows he is a citizen of the world. His crops will travel farther than he will; they will feed the hungry, but also the starving, in countries he will never see. That field he will plow, disc, harrow, fertilize, plant, cultivate, may ultimately keep alive people of a different skin, language, culture, surviving in their remote landscapes or massive cities because he works that nourishing, black soil.

One of the most concentrated sources of food is the corn kernel (the soybean comes close, but has less variety of items in its richness). In that miniature factory are starch, protein, and oil. Beginning as a vigorous grass, corn has been developed by genetic ingenuity (much of it at Iowa State University) into a rugged plant on which one ear may have hundreds of life-sustaining kernels. First came "hybrid" varieties, doubling the yield per acre. The newest is "high lysine" corn (lysine is an amino acid) which can greatly increase the protein content.

The "Corn Belt" is a very accurate phrase to describe that Midwestern area of which Iowa is the center. If one symbol to represent the state had to be chosen, it should be the tough corn plant, with its stalk so devoted to growth that roots come out of the base and go down into the soil. Its broad green leaves glisten. At night, in sweltering August, the rustling of leaves seems to be the sound of growing.

Every kid knows popcorn, the little kernel which explodes into the movie-munching sound. There is sweet corn, its natural sweetness heightened with butter at the dinner table. There is field corn, the basic hog and cattle feed which is eaten after being converted into marbled meat. It is these plants which make Iowa the heart of the heartland, which make the farm center of the United States into the food center of the world.

Some of the most complicated mixtures are in the feeds which are given not to people but to animals. One hog chow contains, among other ingredients, soybeans, buttermilk, yeast, fish, sugar, corn, limestone, zinc, cobalt, acetate, linseed oil, rolled oats, fish liver, manganese sulphate, vitamins, antibiotics, riboflavin. Children eating prepared breakfast cereals do not eat such a beautifully balanced combination as pigs in a stinking barnyard.

Fertility in Iowa is not confined to the basic dirt from which life grows. It pervades the imagination in the arts also. The University of Iowa was the first in the United States (and perhaps in the world) to accept creative work in all the arts as a natural part of a student's work. The Pulitzer Prize, the National Book Award, the Lamont Award (first manuscripts of poetry), inclusion in the Yale Series of Younger Poets — they have all come to University of Iowa people out of all proportion to enrollment. Music resounds at all the state's colleges and universities, space is given to the painter, the sculptor, the printmaker, the composer, the playwright. The astonishing aspect of this care for the arts is not, however, its abundance, but its sophistication; the artist from New York, Paris, Warsaw, Tokyo, Bucharest feels as much at home in Iowa as in his own country. He might even feel more welcome in Iowa, which searches out talent

Overleaf: North Iowa Band Festival held every June in Mason City, with hundreds of high school bands participating. Meredith Willson often returns to his hometown to act as bandmaster. (IDC photograph.)

and gives it a congenial recognition not always found widely in this wicked world.

Iowa has traditionally had the highest literacy rate of all the states. It also has a high number of colleges: Coe, Grinnell, Cornell, Luther, Wartburg, Clarke, Iowa Wesleyan, Loras, Morningside, Simpson, Upper Iowa, St. Ambrose, William Penn, Marycrest, Graceland, Central, Buena Vista, Waldorf, Westmar, Mount Mercy, Grand View. They bring the chance of education to every part of the state, as do its universities: Iowa, Iowa State, Northern Iowa, Drake. It is fascinating to find that the people go on taxing themselves to support public institutions, or giving of their own resources (seldom huge) to private institutions. You fertilize to enhance the fertility of your fields, so why not also raise the human level of your citizens?

Yet there are problems. In the decade of the sixties, seventy-four of Iowa's ninety-nine counties lost population, although Polk, Linn, and Scott gained because they contain the cities of Des Moines, Cedar Rapids, and Davenport-Bettendorf. The number of persons over seventy-five increased by twenty-two per cent, while the number under four years of age declined twenty-four per cent. The young people leave because there are not enough jobs (and those leaving are often the brightest and best-educated in the professions). Many of the old are staying because retirement to traditional places like California is not as urgent when houses can be made so much more comfortable. Farmers will retire to the county seat town instead of Long Beach.

But the basic decency of the people has been constant throughout its history. These are men and women for whom "work" is not a dirty four-letter word. They are good persons in a rewarding landscape. When two men fought with knives in the State Capitol building in the last century, the Governor came out and courteously asked them not to spill blood on the new carpet because it belonged to the taxpayers. When Ralph, a slave, was caught in Iowa after escaping from the south, a farmer quit his fields and went to his aid, insisting that he remain free because any man should be free. The farm boy makes a good industrial worker because he has handled and repaired machinery all his life. Tennessee Williams, while a student at the University of Iowa, was able to eat because he worked in the Iowa Memorial Union cafeteria, serving some of the same people who later saw his plays. When the Cedar Rapids painter Marvin Cone needed a year away from teaching at Coe College, to give all his time to painting, a group of local businessmen collected a fund and sent him to Mexico, where he produced more art than in his previous five years. In a state basically conservative, great risks are taken on innovative people, because what is being conserved is the value of the human race, not just property.

This liberal-conservative attitude is present in the Des Moines *Register,* the state's morning paper, and in the Cedar Rapids *Gazette,* both of which give a remarkable amount of valuable space to the arts, as well as to international and national news. Coming back from a trip around the world, I find the Iowa newspaper reader better informed about the world than the citizens of most other countries, and given a wider range of editorial points of view than he would get from many metropolitan newspapers of far greater circulation in some of the world's major cities. It is all a part of that regard for the individual which permeates the state, and has shaped its history.

Like many other states once agricultural, Iowa has now industrialized. Its largest employer is John Deere Company, a corporation as imaginative as the state's universities. A farmer can now buy a four-wheel-drive tractor with power steering, soft seat, radio and tape deck, lights, and hydraulic equipment which allows him to raise and lower implements which plant or cultivate or harvest twelve rows at a time while he sits comfortably inside an air-conditioned cab. In this lucky land between the two great rivers, there is a happy blending of the most ancient craft of putting seed in soil and the most modern skill in making machines which enormously expand the power of the hand to produce the food and fiber by which all men live. "Nothing runs like a Deere" is the company slogan, accompanied by a graceful, leaping deer. Unlike so many corporate phrases, this one is true. It is a comfort to know that Iowa builds the machines which make their green way across the green fields.

The state has come a long way from the nineteenth century rime:

> Mush is rough,
> Mush is tough,

Thank Thee, Lord,
We've got enough.

Its rough climate produces a kind people. The days of bitter wind biting through the heaviest clothes are matched by days in spring when the air itself seems as nourishing as the food in the field. There are autumn days when the leaves burn with the sun's own colors. When a farmer falls ill or is injured at harvest time, words run over the telephone, the neighbors bring over their great machines and pick hundreds of acres of his corn in a single day. Men make machines serve man, the most valuable and enriching process in the world.

Iowa has always tolerated all varieties of ideas, people, and weather. The Amish have been allowed to keep their own schools, which did not conform to state educational law. The Amana villages west of Iowa City have been permitted to make their own religion and their own social order. Beginning with total, idealistic communal ownership of all means of production, even of the houses their people lived in, believing that God still spoke in a human voice to their little community (He spoke an eighteenth-century Hessian German!), they were allowed without interference to shape their lives into the combined private-cooperative manner of today. So did the Hungarians following Louis Kossuth find a home in northwestern Iowa, the Dutch at Pella, the Norwegians at Decorah, the Swiss and French and Irish and English, the Czechs at Cedar Rapids.

In the midst of the complexities and disasters of the twentieth century, Iowa has kept its old attitudes while adapting to the always-changing now. Walk the county fairs, the state fair, and see the survival of crops and animals in the midst of the gaudy midway. The 4-H girls and boys braid horse manes and comb steer tails by day and dance to the latest rock at night. The hogs and cattle parade before the judges, their hides given more careful treatment than the skins of the farmers showing them. The single and most Iowa-based point is this: No matter how superb the animals may *look*, the final moment of truth comes when they are slaughtered and the carcass is hung up for inspection. The loin eye is measured. The animals display their feeding, their breeding, their fundamental quality. It is that deep concern for quality, in machine, in creature, in person, which the word IOWA means.

There is quality in life here; open space, most of the sky clean, little great wealth, little harsh poverty. A middle life in the middle of the country. There are summer days when the humid air hangs still and heavy on the human head, when the body seems to be nourished not by plant or animal fiber, but from the simple act of breathing. Here man nourishes fields, and in fair return they nourish man. This is what Iowa is all about: Nourishing the curious, beautiful, desperate human race.

ROCK

Pilot Rock near Cherokee, Cherokee County, is a huge glacial boulder of quartzite. It was known to the Indians as Woven Stone and was used as a point of departure for many Indian trails. The early pioneers also found it useful as a landmark before the first roads were built. (IDC photograph.)

Pilot Knob, in Pilot Knob State Park, Hancock and Winnebago counties. The knob, left by the last glacier some 50,000 years ago, rises some 300 feet above the surrounding valley. It was a landmark to navigate by on the rolling plains, and today from the 40-foot stone tower a larger area of fertile land may be viewed than from anywhere else in Iowa. (IDC photograph.)

Stone City in Jones County has really had two lives. One as a boom town began in 1850 when John A. Green settled there and started the first quarry.
By 1900 the town was dying when increased use of cement and other building materials cut the need for stone. In 1930 Grant Wood turned it into an
artists' colony. Today the quarry is once again in profitable operation, as are
a number of others along the Wapsipinicon River. (UofI Archives photograph.)

Rock has always been important to Iowa life. Before the first white
man set foot on Iowa soil the Indians stampeded buffalo off high
limestone cliffs, carved pictographic symbols in red sandstone, and
made axheads and arrowheads from the quartzite at Gitchie
Manitou. Julien Dubuque founded Iowa's oldest town in 1788 when
he began working lead deposits. During the early part of the nineteenth century the lead mines were still producing four to six
million pounds of ore annually. *Iowa: The Home for Immigrants*, states in
1870: "There is no scarcity of good building stone to be found
along nearly all the streams east of the Des Moines River, and
along that stream from its mouth up to the north line of Hum-
boldt county."

This stone barn on Highway 218, just north of Nashua, sits beside a stone dwelling with a stone carriage house — undoubtedly all of them built entirely from the rock of a nearby hill.

Turkey River Bridge, Elkader, Clayton County. The old stone arch bridge over the Turkey River was completed in 1889. It is one of the finest and longest stone arch highway bridges west of the Mississippi. With the exception of an outside sidewalk built in 1924 the bridge has remained unchanged since it was finished.

Main Amana, Iowa County. This house is one of many in the seven villages built by communal labor from the native stone.

Pioneer Rock Church in the ghost village of Ceres, between Guttenberg and Garnavillo on Highway 52, Clayton County, was built in 1858 from stone quarried nearby. No longer used for regular services, it is now a landmark furnished much as it was in pioneer days with short-back pews, a pulpit with winding stairs, the old organ, and a stove.

Anamosa Prison was built by convict labor with stone quarried in Stone City and was completed early in this century.

Fort Atkinson, Winneshiek County, was built in 1840 at the request of the Winnebago Indians to protect them from the Sioux. In 1848 the Winnebagos were moved to a new reservation. The fort was abandoned in 1849 and settlers found its limestone a ready source of building materials. A blockhouse, a powder magazine, and part of one barracks survived.

Cobblestone Alley, Burlington, Iowa. Built on a bluff on the Mississippi River, this town used the natural resources available to it. Since the hill was of limestone easily quarried, many of the town's early streets were paved with it. Cobblestone Alley is the only remaining such street.

The old Nazarene Church in Burlington was built in 1868 as a German Lutheran church using limestone block quarried from the hill at the back of the site. Its loft area is supported by eighteen-inch native oak beams. After being unused for a number of years, it has been acquired by the Art Guild for restoration and use as a community art center.

WATER

This view of the Mississippi evokes the lonely feeling of the river without people — of the river as Marquette and Joliet saw it on June 17, 1673.

In 1973, the new "Marquette" and "Joliet" reenacted the journey of 300 years before. The two are shown as they came up the Iowa River to land for the first time on Iowa soil at today's Toolesboro and to discover evidence of human habitation.

Sergeant Floyd Monument on the bank of the Missouri River. The first registered National Historical Landmark in the United States, the stone obelisk was erected in 1900 to mark the grave of Sergeant Charles Floyd, the only person to die on the Lewis and Clark expedition of 1804-06. (IDC photograph.)

Heralding a new era of expansion for the United States, Thomas Jefferson purchased the Louisiana Territory from France and ordered Captain Meriwether Lewis and William Clark to explore this new land. The Missouri provided a natural highway. Iowa's history is full of stories of the men who traveled the state's almost 15,000 miles of rivers and streams. Trappers learned from the Indians that all they need do was burn the center out of a large tree to provide themselves with a waterworthy craft. A few logs lashed together made a serviceable raft for transporting things downriver. Soon keel boats and barges carrying two sailing masts and as many as fifty oarsmen were plying Iowa rivers. The *Western Engineer* became the first steamship to reach Council Bluffs on the Missouri in 1819, and within twenty years many of Iowa's rivers were alive with the sounds of steamboat whistles.

Geese on the Missouri flyway. Both the Missouri and the Mississippi River
are on the migration path of ducks, geese, and other birds.

A number of seagulls make themselves at home along the Mississippi.

Restored grist mill on Pine Creek in what is now Wild Cat Den State Park.
The mill was built in 1850 by Benjamin Nye and remained in operation until 1927. Besides supplying plantation owners in the south with wheat flour
to feed slaves, the mill was also the site of the first store and post office in
Muscatine County.

The *Rhodedendron* came to Iowa in 1966 when the Clinton County Historical Society bought the 193-foot showboat from the State of West Virginia. It was refurbished and is both a museum and a theater during the summer months. In the early steamboat days, even entertainment arrived by boat. *The Rhododendron* captures the feeling of the old showboats. You can stand on the promenade deck, where the band played as the ship steamed into port. You can walk past gilded mirrors that decorate the walls and see a performance of one of the old melodramas where heroes were heroes and villains twirled their black mustaches.

Views of Bentonsport from the Des Moines River and of its old post office, perhaps the earliest in Iowa still surviving. Mark Twain sailed steamboat routes to Keokuk, where he set type for his brother's newspaper and tried his hand at writing. It was probably there he first met Albert Bigelow Paine, who eventually was to be Twain's first biographer. Paine lived in the river boom town of Bentonsport, about fifteen miles up the Des Moines from Keokuk.

The old Hotel Manning at Keosauqua, the Van Buren County seat, laid out in 1839.

Millions of tons of heavy cargo are shunted up and down the Mississippi and Missouri rivers much more efficiently than on any man-made highway. For example, corn and soybeans from Iowa are taken to New Orleans and from there transshipped to ports around the world.

The *George M. Verity* is an old paddlewheel towboat. It began modern barge service between St. Louis, Missouri, and St. Paul, Minnesota, and was one of the last sternwheelers to operate on the Mississippi. The boat was given to the city of Keokuk by the Armco Steel Company and has been maintained as a river museum.

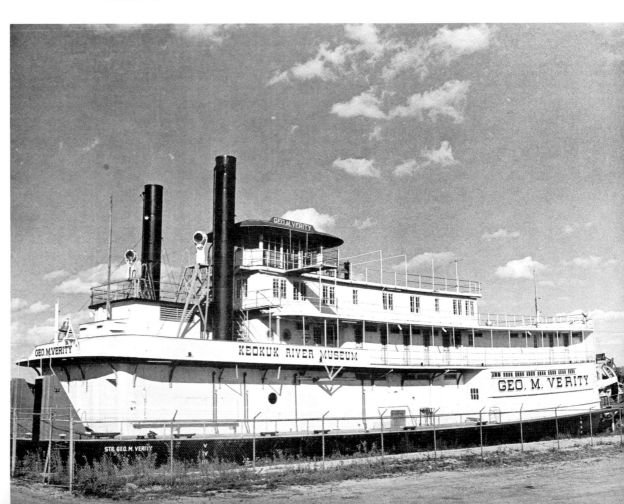

Children at Iowa City park. Because of the abundance of water in Iowa many cities and towns have their own small lakes. This one is used in winter for ice skating and other activities as well as for fishing in summer.

Below: Lake Okoboji. This lake and Spirit Lake in Dickinson are known as the Iowa Great Lakes. They were formed by a glacier about 12,500 years ago. West Okoboji Lake is regarded by many as one of the three most beautiful blue water lakes in the world.

Opposite page: Yellow River Forest in Allamakee features trout streams in a 5,610-acre, multiple-use recreation area.

Members of the University Sailing Club sailing for pleasure in a stiff breeze on Lake McBride. The boats are also used for sailing instruction in coed physical education classes. The club competes in the Midwest Collegiate Sailing Association.

Below: The dam at Coralville Reservoir, of which Lake McBride is a part, is one of a series of flood control dams.

Opposite page: Lake Keomah, near Oskaloosa in Mahaska County, is in a 366-acre park. Almost no Iowan is more than fifty miles from one of Iowa's many small natural lakes or the increasing number of man-made ones.

Opposite, below: Red Haw State Park, near Chariton in Lucas County, named for trees that grow in the area.

Streaking toward a farm pond.

Fishing for pond-raised catfish.

Opposite page: Clear Lake, near Mason City in Cerro Gordo County, is one of Iowa's glacially formed lakes and is 6 miles long by 2½ miles wide. Spring-fed, it was a favorite camping ground of the Sioux and Winnebago during the summer months. Today it is a major recreation area not only for Iowans, but for tourists.

FARMLAND

Kalsow Prairie, near Manson in Pocahontas County, is one of the few isolated places where the virgin prairie still exists. Some 230 species that represent at least 35 different plant families have been found there. (IDC photograph.)

These oxen are part of the Orange City Tulip Festival in Sioux County. The prairie sod, undisturbed for thousands of years, needed a large steel plow and often twenty and more oxen if it was to be broken up for planting. After the first year it could be plowed with smaller teams. (IDC photograph.)

Preceding pages: Amish farmers in Johnson County race to get hay before a summer storm in much the same way as did early Iowa farmers, depending on a good team of horses and a strong back to see them through.

Deer in Washington County, photographed by Mike Jones. In early days deer supplied meat for a family that was trying to conserve its own animals.

The first settlers found life on the prairie formidable. Men drowned crossing rivers, froze in blizzards, were killed in falls from horses, by Indian arrows and white men's bullets. What would be just a scratch today, often killed then. Grass, tall as a horse, rotted and made the soil rich, but it could hide unseen dangers; sometimes it caught fire and, running faster than a horse, consumed fence, cabin — people.

Despite the dangers they came, some by boat, and thousands more in prairie schooners by the overland route. A few had money, but in most cases the team, the wagon, and the wagon's contents represented the total of the family's worldly possessions. Arthur Springer, in his *History of Louisa County*, states: "Each brought with him an axe and augur, a froe [a tool used to split wood for clapboards and shingles] and mallet, a plow, a log chain, and a shovel." The covered wagon provided transportation by day, and lodging by night — and the journey often required two months from the East.

Living History Farms, near Des Moines. The two photographs are of the recreated farm of about 1840, another is a Horse and Steam Engine Farm of about 1900, and the final one to be built here will be a farm of the future. This nonprofit development is designed to portray agriculture in Iowa from its beginnings.

From what nature provided these pioneers built: raw oak became split rail fencing to hold in the livestock or shingles for the roof. Native stone and mud were used as chinking for the gaps between logs in the cabin walls, and for the fireplace. Hickory and cherry wood were gathered for the smoking of meats. Nearby streams could provide fish and fresh water. Once the necessities of shelter were taken care of they began thinking of taming the wilderness. Soon it was time for bridge building. Felling the tallest trees, the pioneers began throwing bridges across the most manageable streams, building ferryboats for others. Before long, Iowa was on its way toward civilization.

Amish farmers haul firewood.

You had no choice but to live with your environment in the early days. If the weather didn't cooperate, you waited patiently for better times. "The winter is generally dry," wrote Lieutenant Albert M. Lea, one of the first white men to visit Iowa, "the waters are all bridged with ice; the snow is frequently deep enough to afford good sleighing; and it is considered the best season for traveling...every prairie is a high road."

Many Iowa farmers from then until the recent past made ample use of sleigh and sled. On many farms you will find one sitting in a corner, covered with dust, hay, and chicken manure. During the

winter months, it was possible to haul heavy loads over firm ground with far less effort than in other seasons. Dead trees in wooded areas could be sledded in to provide a winter's fuel supply, or for building come spring. A barn dance, a sewing or quilting bee, or a neighborly visit was only a sleighride away.

Natural refrigeration was available on any farm or just a short drive away. Rivers, lakes, and ponds provided good places from which to cut huge blocks of ice, to be packed in ice houses as refrigeration for meats and vegetables, or to be ground with cream and vanilla to make ice cream. In a good ice house, winter ice could last until the following September or October when new vegetables were ready and cooling breezes heralded the coming of winter again.

Members of Iowa's Old Order Amish sect still gather in the winter to cut ice from unpolluted farm ponds.

Loading ice. These cakes of ice can weigh from 150 to 200 pounds.

As wagons are filled they are hauled to the various Amish farms that still make use of ice houses.

Opposite page: Farm scene in Johnson County.

Farming methods in use today in Iowa span more than half a century. The Old Order Amish still find the old-fashioned ways best. Other farmers prefer more modern methods. (Bottom photograph from John Deere Company.)

Amish farm with a blend of past and present methods of farming. The Amish still regard rubber tires on tractors as being too modern and replace them with steel rims.

Opposite page: Cornfield and barn near Wapello, in Louisa County.

Iowa has a thriving dairy industry utilizing the most modern equipment. The Amish girl prefers the hand method, but another farm family of Amish descent has an almost totally automated dairy barn, with automatic floor sweepers, special collars on the cows to give more food to the ones that produce more milk, and so much sterile glass that one is reminded of a hospital laboratory.

Dairy herd in Johnson County.

Beef cattle in Washington County.

The Amish carry on an old Iowa tradition, the barn raising.

Opposite page, at top: Octagonal barn on the Wayne Roberts farm, Route 3, Iowa City. Almost ninety years old, the barn was built by Roberts' grandfather, who came to Iowa from Wales.

Opposite page, lower left: Round barn built around 1920 by Joseph Miller near Hills, Iowa.

Opposite page, lower right: Brick barn built by Mennonite Joseph P. Gingerich in 1931 in Johnson County.

In the first years after areas of Iowa became relatively settled and the crops were in, the barn raisings began. Every neighbor for miles around came to lend a hand. It was a day of picnicking and fun for the kids, coupled with a few light chores such as carrying water to the men. For the women it was a time of visiting while they prepared food for all.

The first Iowa barns had hand-hewn timbers and joinings made with wooden pegs rather than nails. Itinerant carpenters often helped to put up the main framing, but the farmer himself usually put on the finishing touches to suit himself. The state's barns reflect the diversity of cultural background of its farmers. There are barns that suggest an early New England background, with stone foundations; the huge Pennsylvania-style ones for bountiful harvests; the rotund German barns in every size; round barns credited to the Shaker Movement, and of which it was said that the devil could find in them no corner in which to hide; the octagonal; the square . . .

Opposite page: Barn on hillside in Louisa County. Although many people think of Iowa as flat, it has numerous hilly areas. In this case it was probably preferable to put the barn here and use the best land for corn.

Much farm equipment is manufactured in Iowa — for example the John Deere tractor (bottom) made in Waterloo with a front-mounted cultivator made in the Des Moines plant. (Above, IDC photograph. Below, John Deere Company photograph.)

Harvesting corn. (John Deere Company photograph.)

Although horses no longer play a primary role in farm life for anyone save the Amish, they are still to be found on many Iowa farms.

PEOPLE

Effigy Mounds, near Marquette, in Allamakee and Clayton counties. There are over 191 prehistoric Indian mounds in the two-square-mile area of this national monument.

Archeological evidence shows the Indians arrived in Iowa by at least 10,000 B.C.; it is suspected they came 10,000 years earlier. In the span of the last 10,000 years there have been many Indian cultures in Iowa. The Oneota culture, at its high point, turned to artistry, making designs on pottery and other utensils and inscribing stone tablets. In modern history there were thirteen Indian tribes in the state. Today the only significant Indian culture in Iowa is the Mesquakie (known to many as the Sac and Fox) near Tama in Tama County.

An Indian family group sits on a porch, while other members of the tribe gather around the home for a religious ceremony taking place in the traditional wickiup behind the house.

Following two pages: Members of the tribe in full ceremonial regalia during the Pow Wow.

The young ones, one foot in old Indian ways, the other in modern political activism.

An old dancer at the Mesquakie Indian Pow Wow at the settlement near Tama. The Pow Wow today is an occasion for tribal unity and for continuing Indian traditions; it has also become a political caucus between various Indian tribes to discuss the "Indian Power" movement.

Overall view of many of the tribal family gathered for the religious ceremony. Approximately 1,500 Mesquakies live on or near the 3,600-acre settlement.

The Amish and the Indian are both earth cultures, with roots in the land. The Mesquakie returned clandestinely to Iowa after being sent to a Kansas reservation and bought back some of their own lands from the white man in the last century.

The Amish came to Iowa around the 1840's, at about the same time the Indians were returning to it. The Amish were seeking religious freedom and the right to live as they chose. Today their ways stand out more prominently. The Amish girl (right) wears the kind of dress they maintain. This girl, as do about half the Amish children, later chose to live in the modern world. After she was twenty-one, she married a non-Amish man and went "gay," as the Amish say of those who go out in the world. The old man on the opposite page has remained staunchly Amish — no electricity, no telephone, no modern farm machinery or transportation. There are no curtains in the windows and no decorations in the house.

Born out of the religious turmoil of the Anabaptist movement in
sixteenth-century Switzerland, the Amish came to America in a
search for freedom from persecution. Today in Iowa they can be
found near Kalona, Independence, Oelwein, and Milton. They still
speak the German dialect their forebears brought with them when
they came to this country before the American Revolution. In recent years they have built new one-room schools where their children can learn in German as well as English, thanks to a ruling by
the United States Supreme Court which gave the Amish the right
to educate their children according to their own beliefs. They be-
lieve in schooling only through the eighth grade.

A Sunday visit is very much a part of
the Amish way of life, along with
barn raisings, picnics, and auctions.

Here an Amishman talks with friends
and fellow graduates of Middleburg
School, a one-room public school that
had been in operation more than fifty
years and only recently closed.

Amish girls head into Kalona for some Saturday shopping. Kalona is still very much a Saturday farm town, and the hitch rails behind its grocery store are usually filled with buggies from early morning to noon.

The two barefoot girls wear perfect examples of the Amish dress. The little girl wearing the prayer cap has obviously hung her bonnet up nearby.

An array of the many meats smoked in the 100-year-old smokehouse of the Homestead Meat Shop in Homestead, part of the seven Amana villages. Hams, sausage, and meals in the Ox Yoke Inn and Ronenburg's have helped make Amana food famous throughout Iowa.

What makes Amana significant is its religious life. As with the Amish, the basic language is German. Unlike the Amish, the Amana villages do have a church — a very plain building. Women are leaving after German services in the church at Amana.

Jack Hahn, who operates the Hahn Bakery in Middle Amana, is following a profession as old as Amana itself. The bakery dates back to the days of the Amana communal society when meals were cooked and served in communal style.

Mrs. Alma Ehrle of the Ehrle Brothers Winery started the first winery in the Amanas in 1938; here she shows wines she produces in the basement of her home in Homestead. The four kinds of wines produced — rhubarb, white and dark grape, and strawberry — are naturally fermented and aged.

Arthur Miller, Mrs. Ehrle's son-in-law, makes rhubarb wine in the hand-operated tradition that still prevails in the Amanas.

Mrs. Susannah Rettig, a life-long resident of Middle Amana, often led tours of the area. In her later years, she did a number of television commercials, something she always laughed about because "they were easier than really doing the cooking."

Interior of the Amana church.

Russian Easter Procession at St. John's Eastern Orthodox Church in Cedar Rapids. Easter is celebrated according to the Greek calendar. One of the most colorful parts of the service is the handing out of the blessed Easter eggs first to all the children in the congregation and then to the adults.

Opposite page: Cedar Rapids has also long been the home of Czech immigrants and their descendants. Many of Cedar Rapids' street signs were long set forth in both English and Czech although today only Little Bohemia (Sixteenth Avenue in Cedar Rapids) still has such signs. A Czech school was begun 104 years ago. Today the Czech language is still being taught to children by volunteer teachers.

The Sykora Bakery during Czech Heritage Day.

Women gather for a street dance in Cedar Rapids.

Street dancing continues to midnight during the Czech neighborhood's celebration of its traditions.

New Melleray Abbey, ten miles southwest of Dubuque off U.S. Highway 151, was founded in 1849 by monks from County Waterford, Ireland. Even today a number of the monks come from Ireland. The Trappists eat no meat and follow a vow of silence, living under a discipline that has prevailed for over a thousand years.

The lighting-of-the-fire ceremony at Easter. All candles and other lights are extinguished, a bonfire is lighted outside, and from that bonfire the Pascal Candle is lighted and from that a candle held by each of the monks — so symbolizing the rebirth of Christ.

Sunday services at the Abbey.

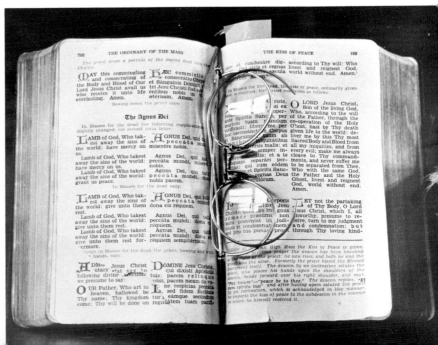

St. Donatus was settled by French-speaking people from Luxemburg and was the site of St. Mary's Academy, the first girls' boarding school in Iowa. The area was also the site of a battle between two warring Indian tribes who threw the bodies off the high cliffs. (IDC photograph.)

The small white church high on a hill, near Old Man's Creek off Highway 1 south of Iowa City, is a monument to the first Welsh settlers in Johnson County. Not only has the First Welsh Congregational Church remained independent, but each July it is the site of an annual homecoming, with former members returning to attend Welsh services and sing the old Welsh songs. Founded in 1846, the church had no building until 1856, and the present one was built in 1871. Membership started declining in the 1930's and in 1950 the last regular services were held, but the homecomings continued and in 1971 enthusiasm ran so high that the church was re-opened.

The town of Pella abounds in such names as Van Zee, De Haan, and Steenhoek. Stop any child on the street and say "Goeden morgen," and he or she will probably answer in Dutch. This little Dutch-settled community has not forgotten its beginnings and through the years its people have maintained close ties with the homeland. Each May, the town celebrates its heritage with the Tulip Festival. Pella was settled in 1847 by 700 Hollanders under the leadership of Reverend Hendrik Pieter Scholte. After crossing the Atlantic they came by steamboat to Keokuk and walked the 200-odd miles to what was to become Pella, many still in their wooden shoes.

Decorah is the largest Norwegian settlement in Iowa. The Nordic Fest was begun by the Norwegian-American Museum in Decorah and the Junior Chamber of Commerce in 1966. (Photograph, left, by Barbara Hartman; below, by Duane Crock, Cedar Rapids *Gazette.*)

Senator Harold Hughes, who served three successive terms as Governor before his election to Congress. Hughes was only the seventh Democratic governor in one hundred seventeen years of statehood.

Novelist Vance Bourjaily and his daughter Robin. Bourjaily, a member of the Writers Workshop at the University of Iowa, not only has won recognition for his own work, but has seen to it that talented beginning writers are encouraged and published.

Mt. Pleasant in Henry County is best known for its annual Midwest Old Settlers' and Threshers' Reunion, but it is also the home of Iowa Wesleyan College, founded in 1842, one of the first American colleges to provide opportunities for women and black students. The college graduated the first woman lawyer in the United States, Belle Babb Mansfield, in 1866, and, in 1935, James Van Allen. Van Allen, who is head of the Department of Physics and Astronomy at the University of Iowa, discovered the Van Allen radiation belts in 1958 and, along with other members of the department, is an important contributor to the United States space program. Under his direction, equipment for such projects as the Mariner probe and the recent Pioneer series launched to Jupiter have been built at the University. (Van Allen: UofI photograph by Warren Paris.)

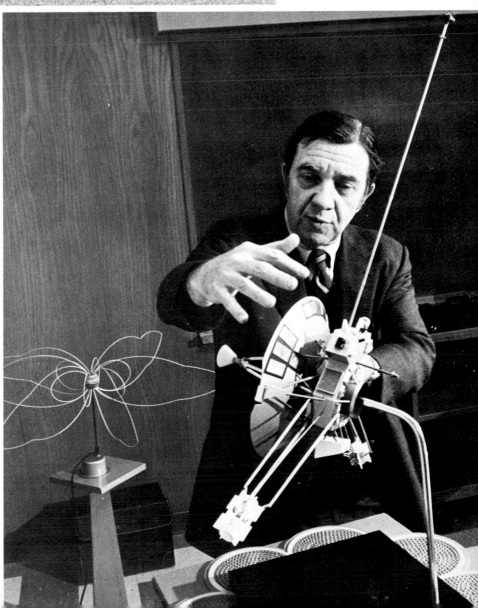

State Senator Minnette F. Doderer, Democrat from the 17th Senatorial District. Born in Grundy County and a graduate of the University of Iowa, Mrs. Doderer lives in Iowa City with her husband and two daughters. She is one of four women among the fifty-one Iowa senators.

Muscatine was one of Iowa's early river towns and, in the days before plastics, a center for the pearl button industry supplied by clams from the Mississippi River. Today, it is noted for its melons and for cucumbers and other vegetables, particularly those grown on the 27,000-acre "island" of sand and gravel formed by the river when it changed channels. Much of this crop is harvested by Chicanos, many of whom have settled in the area, and the local radio station provides regular Spanish-language broadcasts. The street area shown is undergoing some renovation, which is typical of many towns intent on preserving the town square.

George Garcia, a Chicano born in a Laredo, Texas barrio, now teaches high school in Iowa City and is chairman of the Iowa Civil Rights Commission and second vice-president of the Official Human Rights Agencies. A graduate of the University of Iowa, he is at work on a series of television documentaries on the history of the Chicano in eastern Iowa and western Illinois.

While Iowa has long had a relatively small black population, it has not been an "invisible" minority. Iowa State University gave George Washington Carver his first faculty position, and earlier Simpson College had accepted him as a student when a college in Kansas refused him admission. The girl with the motorcycle and the two below are residents of Des Moines.

When members of United Press International struck in the spring of 1974, the Des Moines office was picketed as were its counterparts elsewhere.

Student strike at the University of Iowa in May, 1971.

Drum Major Vern Windsor leads the Hawkeye Marching Band during half-time at the University of Iowa's Nile Kinnick Stadium. (UofI photograph by Warren Paris.)

A young couple.

From territorial days, Iowa was interested in education and it passed legislation in 1838 to provide for "seminaries of learning" in the areas of literature and science. Today the state has the highest literacy rate in the nation and is home to twenty-eight private four-year colleges and universities, three state universities, and twenty-two private and public community and junior colleges. While the modern classroom with the latest in electronic equipment is part of many schools, the one-room school-house is still in existence, used primarily by the Old Order Amish. (Above: UofI photograph by Phyllis Lehrman.)

Mrs. Elizabeth Stumpf, photographed at her one hundredth birthday party in Kalona.

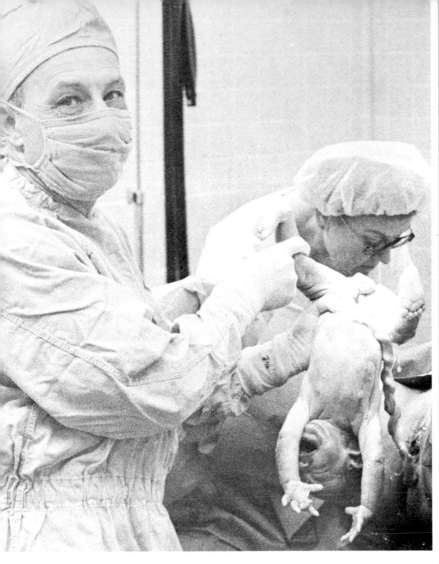

A father and his young son looking at the ants in a city park.

Two girls take a break from shopping in downtown Des Moines.

A rock concert in early May at Lake McBride, where many of the audience sat wrapped in blankets as the weather turned out to be chillier than expected.

A family in Waterloo.

In Madison County, part of Macksburg's population of 142.

Among Iowa's ethnic groups that have maintained strong family ties, such as the Amish and the Indians, and in a traditional religious group like the Trappist Monks, the elderly still play an important role. Respect is paid those whose knowledge and experience will be passed on to future generations.

Many elderly people have given up private dwellings (such as Maggie Brontreger, who maintained one until her nineties) and move to homes such as Pleasantview in Kalona. Operated by the Mennonite Benevolent Association, the home is one of the finest of such facilities.

Independence carries with it the risk of loneliness.

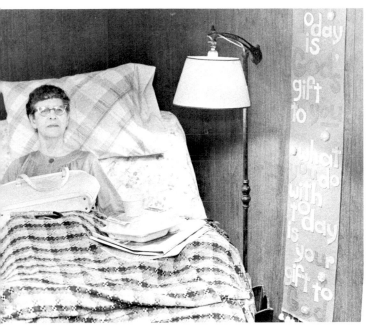

Various agencies in Iowa have become more aware of the problems of the elderly, and many communities now provide the Meals on Wheels service, a program that brings meals to shut-ins (at cost or slightly above, depending on the individual's financial ability). It offers human contact at least once a day. Other areas have a transportation system for the elderly, such as S.E.A.T.S., operated by Kirkwood Community College, Cedar Rapids, which provides inexpensive bus rides to a variety of communities for everything from grocery shopping to social programs.

harles Drollinger, playing the guitar and fiddle, is a participant in Iowa ity's annual Old Fiddlers' Picnic.

HERITAGE

The Old Capitol at Iowa City, now the hub of the University of Iowa, was the state's first permanent capitol. Here the last four Iowa territorial legislatures met, here the transition to statehood took place, here the first state governor was inaugurated and the state constitution drafted. When the seat of government was moved to Des Moines in 1857, the Old Capitol was given to the University as its first home. Ten years before, the University had been chartered in the building by the state's First General Assembly, exactly 59 days after Iowa's final admission to statehood. As the first building owned by the University, the Old Capitol remained both a landmark and housing for the University's central offices for 113 years. Then, in 1970, the University moved out to allow the Old Capitol's restoration as a historic site, and as a simple but excellently designed example of Greek Revival architecture.

The Quakers gave Iowa two of its notable leaders — the only Iowan president, Herbert Hoover, and its first governor, Robert Lucas, appointed to govern the Territory by President Martin Van Buren in 1838. Lucas, who, despite his Quaker background, rose to the rank of colonel in the United States Army, served two terms as the governor of Ohio before he came to Iowa. Lucas was a man well suited to his times: he backed down before nothing. His first year in office was one of constant warring with the legislature and in the second year he contended with Missouri over the southern boundary of Iowa, a controversy which he won. When he left office after a peaceful year, Lucas and his wife bought eighty acres and built Plum Grove, then on the boundary of Iowa City and now on Court Street. It was Lucas's home until his death in 1853. After restoration, it was dedicated in 1946 as a historic site. (IDC photograph.)

Herbert Clark Hoover was born on August 10, 1874, in a whitewashed cottage measuring 14 by 20 feet which was built by his blacksmith father, Jesse Hoover. Early life was not easy for Hoover: his father died when he was six, and at ten he with his brothers was orphaned when their mother died. Despite sporadic pre-college education, he graduated from Stanford University in 1895, having worked his way by doing jobs running from laundryman to paperboy. Trained as a mining engineer, within twenty years he ended this career a multi-millionaire. Instead of simply enjoying the life such wealth afforded, Hoover accepted the job of helping refugees get back to America during World War I, then distributed food to the starving in Europe. The presidency followed eventually. His salaries as a public servant were used to establish scholarships for those who worked for him or to finance research projects for which there was no official budget. Today, the town of West Branch has rebuilt itself around Hoover's life. The Hoover Presidential Library is there and the Quaker Meeting House, where he worshipped, has been restored. The cottage in which he was born is also restored and his father's blacksmith shop is completely functional, as it was a century ago.

The Hoover Presidential Library is laid out as a kind of pictorial biography of the thirtieth president's life. One of the most touching tributes given Hoover were the many flour and grain sacks embroidered by grateful people in Europe. Europeans who remember famine relief still come to honor the man from a small Quaker town who carried Quaker principles to the world.

The "Swinging Bridge," a landmark in Columbus Junction since 1886. It was built first with barrel staves and wire, and these were replaced by a wooden bridge a few years later. The present bridge was restored in 1954, and is a permanent fixture between Third and Fourth streets.

Madison County's well-known covered bridges are found on country roads near Winterset. They served many purposes besides that of a simple crossing. Local merchants used the insides as billboards, couples found them a secluded spot, and circuit-riding ministers often used them as churches in bad weather.

The country's smallest railroad got its start in Dubuque because a local banker hated to miss his after-lunch nap. J.K. Graves had a home on the bluff overlooking the city, which gave him a beautiful view at mid-day, but enjoying the view required a half-hour drive up the hill. Knowledgeable in mechanics as well as money, Graves had a crude cable car built in 1882. Before long, the banker's neighbors began using the car. Not one to pass up a money-making opportunity, the financier charged a nickel per ride, a price that resisted all inflation until 1964, when it was doubled. Today, Graves' railroad still operates, as the Fourth Street Elevator, known also as the Fenelon Place Inclined Railway.

FARE 10¢
HOURS
6:30 A.M. till 11:30 P.M.

E. ELEVATOR CO.

Atop the bluff there is a platform on either side of the engine house that affords a view of Dubuque and the Mississippi River. It is a glimpse into the past: nineteenth-century buildings and other echoes of the Victorians abound. Almost directly below the bluff is St. Raphael's Cathedral and, further, dominating the center of the city, is the massive brick county courthouse. A form of settlement had been in existence there even before 1788, when Julien Dubuque signed a formal agreement with the Indians to mine lead.

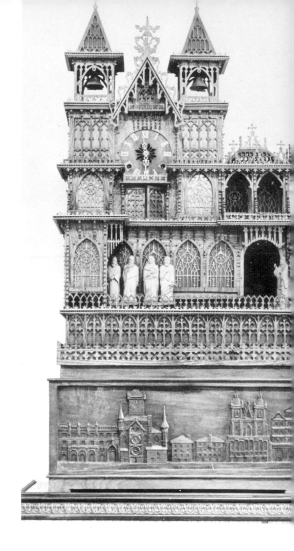

Frank and Joseph Bily, sons of Czech immigrants, lived out their lives on a small northeastern Iowa farm. As children the brothers became interested in carving, to the consternation of their teachers, who kept taking their knives away because the two carved on the desks, and of their farmer father, who found such a hobby a waste of time. But neither teachers nor father stopped them. Despite many offers, the brothers consistently refused to sell even one of the pieces — which range from a cathedral clock with thousands of inlaid pieces of native woods (including the figures of the twelve apostles) to statuary of the famous of Iowa and the world. When the brothers died, their clocks and other carvings were willed to their hometown of Spillville, in Winneshiek County.

The clocks can be seen in the house where the composer Anton Dvořák stayed during his visit to Spillville in 1893. A separate room is dedicated to Dvořák memorabilia, including the organ where it is said he composed part of the *New World* Symphony. He found the community a source of inspiration for his *Humoresque* and played at daily mass in St. Wenceslaus Church.

In northeastern Iowa is the region called "Little Switzerland," where you can stand on high hills and gaze out over miles of dairy farms. It was here the Norwegians came.

The Norwegian-American Museum in Decorah, established in 1877, is one of the oldest and largest immigrant ethnic museums in this country, displaying possessions from the Old World and exhibits of pioneer life. The museum, housed in what was formerly a Norwegian-language publishing house, has acquired two additional buildings in the city's business district.

Porter House Museum. A stately Victorian home in Decorah built by
Adelbert Field, widely known collector, naturalist, and artist.

Typical pioneer cabins on the Luther College campus are part of the
Norwegian-American Museum. The buildings were moved from their
original sites, restored, and furnished with period items. (Luther College
photograph.)

Near Oskaloosa is the Nelson Pioneer Farm and Craft Museum, given to the Mahaska County Historical Society by Roy and Lillian Nelson. Continuously worked from 1844 to 1958, it is preserved to illustrate what early Iowa farm life was like. The house (which replaced a simple cabin) was built in 1852 of native timber and of bricks fired in a nearby kiln. Across from it is the Benjamin Littler cabin, built in 1867 and moved to the site from Bussey. In mid-September, the Museum holds its annual Pioneer Crafts Day, with demonstrations of old-fashioned skills such as spinning, weaving, and candlemaking.

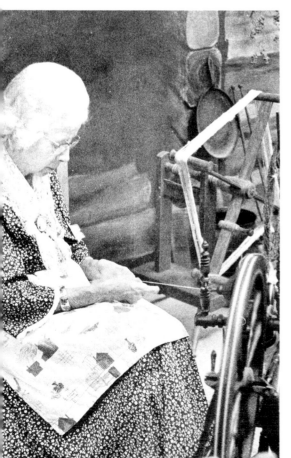

Harlan House, Mt. Pleasant. For sixteen years it was the home of James A. Harlan, president of Iowa Wesleyan College, the first state superintendent of public instruction, and secretary of the interior in the cabinet of President Abraham Lincoln, whose trusted friend he was. Lincoln's son Robert married Harlan's daughter, Mary, in 1868. The couple, with their three children, spent many summers at Harlan House.

Lincoln poster originally painted by Isaac Wetherby of Iowa City for the 1860 Presidential campaign. When Lincoln ran for a second term in 1864, Wetherby simply made a few changes: he added a beard to Lincoln's face, changed the name of his running mate, and altered the slogan to: "Slavery Degrades Labor." The poster is now in the Davenport Museum.

Jonathan Clark Conger House, Washington. Once the showplace of Washington, the Conger House suffered a period of neglect but is being restored by members of the Washington County Historical Society. Its earliest sections date from pre-Civil War days.

The Dodge House in Council Bluffs, a National Landmark, was built by General Grenville Dodge in 1869 and remains one of the finest examples of Victorian architecture in the Midwest. The red exterior vitric brick, the first of its kind used in Council Bluffs, came upriver from St. Louis. The house was visited by Presidents Grant, McKinley, and Theodore Roosevelt, for its owner was the builder of the Union Pacific Railroad. It was Dodge's meeting with President Lincoln in 1859 in Council Bluffs that helped determine Council Bluffs as the eastern terminus for the first transcontinental railroad. Council Bluffs had played an even earlier role in the development of the west as the meeting place of several Indian tribes, and it was here that Brigham Young was appointed head of the Mormon Church in 1847. For several years the Mormon "Frontier Guardian" was published in the city. Ironically, the newspaper's office was located directly across the street from the Ocean Wave Saloon, one of the most notorious in the west. (IDC photograph.)

Salisbury House, Des Moines. This forty-two-room replica of King's House in Salisbury, England, set in eleven acres of woodland, was built by drug and cosmetic manufacturer Carl Weeks between 1923 and 1926, and cost $1.5 million. Its contents include oriental rugs, art objects, and rare books and documents. In the main entrance to the house, the Great Hall, wooden pegs clinch the oak beams of the sixteenth-century ceiling.

The Iowa State Education Association purchased Salisbury House and its contents in 1954 for $200,000 and spent an equal amount renovating and adapting various rooms for offices. However, the ISEA has been careful to keep the House very much as it originally was, and it is open to the public during the day. One of the most valuable items in the House is the portrait of Cardinal Domenico Rivarola by Van Dyck.

ARTS

Designed by Eliel Saarinen, the Des Moines Art Center was dedicated in 1948, having been founded and given to the city by James D. Edmundson. The Center opened an addition, designed by I. M. Pei in 1968. Besides offering a wide range of shows and exhibits of major artists, the center has encouraged beginning artists, many of them native Iowans. Its collection includes works by Goya, Daumier, Pissarro, Courbet, and many of the foremost American artists, including Gilbert Stuart. A junior museum features exhibitions for children. Among its interesting features are the exterior sculpture court and the sculpture gallery.

Two women cast a critical eye at Philip Pearlstein's "Two Female Models Sitting and Lying on a Navajo Rug" (Coffin Fund) in the Des Moines Art Center's main area. At the right is "Maiastra" by Constantin Brancusi (gift of John and Elizabeth Bates Cowles). The lower gallery features Claes Oldenburg's "Three-Way Plug, Scale A (Soft) Prototype in Blue" and Roy Lichtenstein's "The Great Pyramid" (both obtained through the Coffin Fund).

Sculpture court and in background the newly opened room for the Elliott Collection. The Museum of Art at the University of Iowa, on the banks of the Iowa River in Iowa City. One of its greatest gifts is the collection of twentieth-century paintings, silver, and prints given by Mr. and Mrs. Owen Elliott. The Museum was given a Jackson Pollock mural by Peggy Guggenheim and has prints by Mauricio Lasansky, who came to Iowa in 1945 from his native Argentina.

The Blanden Art Gallery, Fort Dodge, has a collection of contemporary art which includes works by Miro, Chagall, Calder, Klee, Kandinsky, Lipchitz. Fort Dodge also has an arts council that holds a yearly festival featuring exhibits, plays, and special programs.

Iowa art is irrevocably linked to Grant Wood, whose best known work is "American Gothic," painted in 1930. Wood did numerous other types of work throughout his career, including interior decorating and the design of the wooden bench shown at the Cedar Rapids Art Center. Although born near Anamosa, a major part of Wood's life and career was spent in Cedar Rapids, where today the Art Center has turned over most of its third floor to its collection of Grant Wood works. In 1927, Wood was commissioned to make the largest stained-glass window in the world as a soldiers' memorial to be placed in the Cedar Rapids Memorial Coliseum. From 1932 to 1934 he had an art colony at Stone City, near Anamosa, because he believed "we need a combination camp and summer art school . . . the Middle West is not covered with the palette scrapings of other painters." His last years, from 1934 until his death in 1942, were spent as a professor at the University of Iowa.

The Davenport Municipal Art Gallery, founded in 1925, was one of the first city-supported art projects in the United States. The present building was opened in 1963. In addition to showing nationally known artists, the gallery has a policy of presenting local and state artists in all media. It also has an important collection of Grant Wood's work and is the only gallery in Iowa that has a significant group of "Old Master" paintings, presented to it at its founding by the late C. A. Ficke.

Above and left: Waterloo has built a Recreation and Arts Center valued at a million dollars with a $250,000 bond issue, $500,000 in individual and group gifts, and donated labor and materials. Truly a community project, the Center is the city's showplace.

Professor Harry Oster, folklorist at the University of Iowa, has spent a decade examining the folk arts and music of Iowa. His house is filled with tools, musical instruments, quilts, and other crafted objects.

Women at Pleasantview Home in Kalona, the Amish-Mennonite-dominated community in Washington County, work on a quilt that will be auctioned during the annual benefit sale for the home.

Snake Alley, in the river city of Burlington, was built in 1894 as a short cut from the hill to the business district. The street with its five half curves and two quarter curves was designed to permit a horse to descend at a normal speed, and the design also prevents the road bed from being washed away. Even the bricks were laid horizontally with uphill edges projecting slightly at an angle to give horses better footing.

The alley is the scene of the local Art Guild's annual exhibit and sale during Steamboat Days. (Burlington Hawk-eye photograph by Lloyd Moffitt.)

Thieves' Markets once were found only on college campuses as places where art students could sell their works. Now art fairs and sales are common happenings at shopping centers, town squares, and city parks all over Iowa.

The Naming, an experimental theater piece of the Iowa Theater Lab, based in Iowa City, has been performed in the United States and Europe. Funded through a grant given to the University of Iowa by the Rockefeller Foundation, the Lab is under the direction of Ric Zank, who has created a highly disciplined and original company. (Photographs by Walt Dulaney.)

The University of Iowa's Stradivari Quartet: Allen Ohmes, violin; Charles Wendt, cello; William Preucil, viola; John Ferrell, violin. Through funds provided by the Iowa Arts Council, the group has presented concerts in Iowa towns as part of the Council's effort to share the state's cultural wealth. (Photograph by University of Iowa News Service.)

Often the creation of an inspired but frustrated poet, the small private press tends to specialize in limited editions of high quality. Kim Merker, who operates the Windhover Press for the University of Iowa and has his own private press, the Stone Wall Press, is nationally known for his fine handset, handbound volumes. Shown are pages from a collection of poems by John Pauker with drawings by Thomas Kovacs, and *Charles Olson in Connecticut*.

LAST LECTURES

As heard by
John Cech
Oliver Ford
Peter Rittner

The Windhover Press
The University of Iowa
Iowa City 1974

And it produces the effect we want,
Our will is done in each particular.
I have nothing but contempt for our weak priest,
The way he acquiesces all the time.
With his collaboration all our purposes
Are served.
          Still I want proof
That he is not playing a double game.

I think the next time he crawls into the grave
I shall shoot. It will create some problems.
We have to live with his parishioners. But
It will clear the air. And we shall see
Whether he is sincere or double-dealing.

excellency:

An overplus of discarded eyeglasses is
Becoming a bother. The frames are of little value,
The lenses ground to prescription.
                    I propose
A decree to require everyone to wear eyeglasses,
Issued at random. Many good angles to this.

Terrace Hill, a fine example of Victorian architecture. Designed by W. W. Beyington, who did the Chicago Water Tower, the mansion was built in Des Moines by financier Benjamin Franklin Allen. When monetary disaster hit Allen, the $250,000 mansion was sold to Frederick M. Hubbell and for eighty-seven years remained the Hubbell family home. In 1971, Hubbell's heirs gave Terrace Hill to the State.

A once private home, now a funeral parlor, in Mt. Pleasant.

The Octagon House in Decorah is one of the few houses in Iowa which is built in the form of an octagon, a style somewhat popular in the eastern states in the 1840's. The walls were of "grout," a mixture of mortar, straw, and small pebbles poured into forms and allowed to harden.

The Blank Performing Arts Center, designed by Charles Herbert of Des Moines, at Simpson College in Indianola. (Photograph by Charles Herbert and Associates.)

C. Y. Stephens Auditorium at Iowa State University in Ames. (Iowa State photograph.)

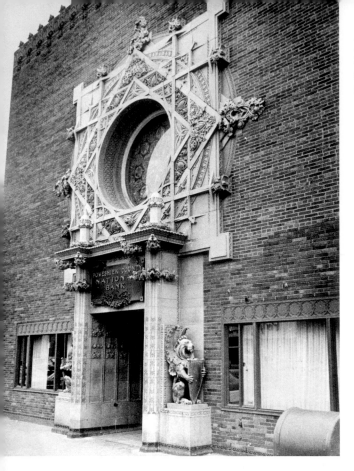

Known as the "Jewel Box," the Poweshiek County National Bank in G[...]nell was designed by Louis Sullivan in 1914. Leader of the late ninetee[...]century "Chicago School," Sullivan developed a personal system of o[...]ment and design based on the shapes of plants and other natural for[...]

The J. G. Melson House in Rock Glen (opposite page), a residential are[...]Mason City. Designed by Walter Burley Griffin in 1912, the dwelling i[...]tirely of rough ashlar and seems to be growing out of the rock. Griff[...]leader of the Prairie School of Architecture, worked with Frank L[...]Wright and is best known for his design of the Australian capital cit[...]Canberra.

Because Mason City was very prosperous in the late nineteenth [...]early twentieth century, many of its leading citizens sought out archi[...]such as Wright and Griffin to design a community that reflected [...]achievement. The result was a planned development that today constit[...]the largest group of Prairie School dwellings in one location.

The Lowell Walter house outside of Quasqueton, north of Cedar Rapids, in Buchanan County, was designed and built by Frank Lloyd Wright along the banks of the Cedar River.

Walter Burley Griffin's house for J. E. Blythe was built in the Rock Glen/Rock Creek area where even the creek has been landscaped. Now owned by Robert E. McCoy, an orthopedic surgeon, the house is part of the community of Prairie architecture in Mason City.

Construction in Cedar Rapids.

Duane Arnold, president and board chairman of Iowa Electric Light and Power, sits at the control center of Iowa's first atomic reactor, near Palo in Linn County.

Overleaf: Power plant at the University of Iowa. (UofI photograph by Drake Hokanson).

Developing procedures to test water quality are Professor Marcus Powell and research assistant Bobbie McDonald of the University of Iowa. Laboratory work is often assisted by a computer, as at the University's computer center. (UofI photographs by Warren Paris.)

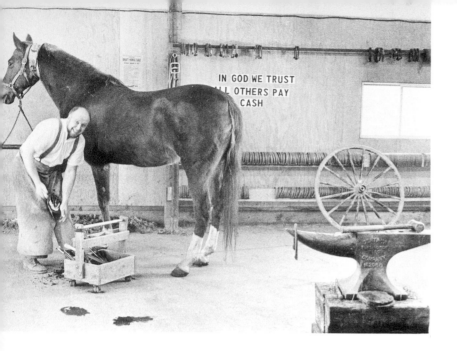

Amish blacksmith William J. Schrock is kept busy in Kalona shoeing horses and repairing buggy wheels.

Mrs. William Kron frequently helps her husband at his service station off Interstate 80 near Iowa City.

This resident of Pleasantview Home in Kalona works almost daily making and repairing items in the home's basement machine shop.

The Quaker Oats plant on the banks
of the Cedar River in Cedar Rapids.
Quaker Puffed Wheat and Quaker
Puffed Rice are literally fired from a
kind of cannon, of which no pictures
are allowed.

Plant at Burlington on the Mississippi River.

John Deere Company operates several plants in Iowa. The firm has head-quarters near Moline, which forms part of the Quad-City area of Daven-port and Bettendorf, Iowa, and Moline and Rock Island, Illinois. Started by a Vermont-born blacksmith, John Deere, who developed the world's first successful steel plow, the company is today the world's largest producer of farm equipment.

Since the days of the first fairs, the fine handiwork of farm wives has been displayed at the many local and county fairs, as well as the State Fair. The quilt and sewing work display is at the Waterloo Cattle Congress, which is one of northeastern Iowa's biggest events of the fall. In 1854 the first State Fair's prizes for the winning exhibits ranged from one to ten dollars and three top fifteen-dollar awards. Admission was twenty-five cents and when all the expenses and premiums were paid, the management had a fifty-dollar profit. This was so encouraging that the Iowa Agricultural Society decided to make the fair an annual event.

Home-canned fruits and vegetables . . . jar after colorful jar displaying blue and red ribbons . . . cattle and swine whose coats and hooves have been given more care than their owners' Sunday best . . . the litany of the carnival barker on the midway . . . this is a climax of the Iowa year: fair time.

Potatoes are among the things judged at the Waterloo Cattle Congress.

Fruits and grains of all types are judged at the State Fair in Des Moines —
from watermelons through the multi-formed squash. (IDC photograph.)

Given a permanent home in Des Moines in 1879, the State Fair had moved around the state for twenty-five years. It was held in Muscatine, Dubuque, and Keokuk, among other towns. (IDC photograph.)

Although the arts and other forms have a place at the fair, it is also a major livestock show and preparation for judging and showing is as thorough and time-consuming as in a theatrical production. (IDC photograph.)

Often the "winner" in the various livestock categories is sold at a top price for beef. Other winners are breeding stock.

For Spencer, the biggest event is the annual Clay County fair, which has been held there since 1871, only five years after the early settlers drove their covered wagons down from Wisconsin to what was called Spencer Grove. Locust plagues in the years following nearly forced the settlers to move, but by 1879 conditions had improved. (IDC photograph.)

In Waterloo, the annual dairy Cattle Congress draws participants from all over Iowa. One of the biggest livestock expositions in the Midwest, it also has one of largest horse shows. Held in October, it marks the end of the fair season in Iowa.

The square dance has been on the fair scene nearly from the beginning. Although the clothes are much fancier and more colorful than those of the early settlers, the music and the steps are still the same. For many of the dancers, fair time means a full circuit of dancing, generally in competition and for awards, starting in midsummer and finishing in the fall.

The carnival midway is now a large part of nearly all fairs.

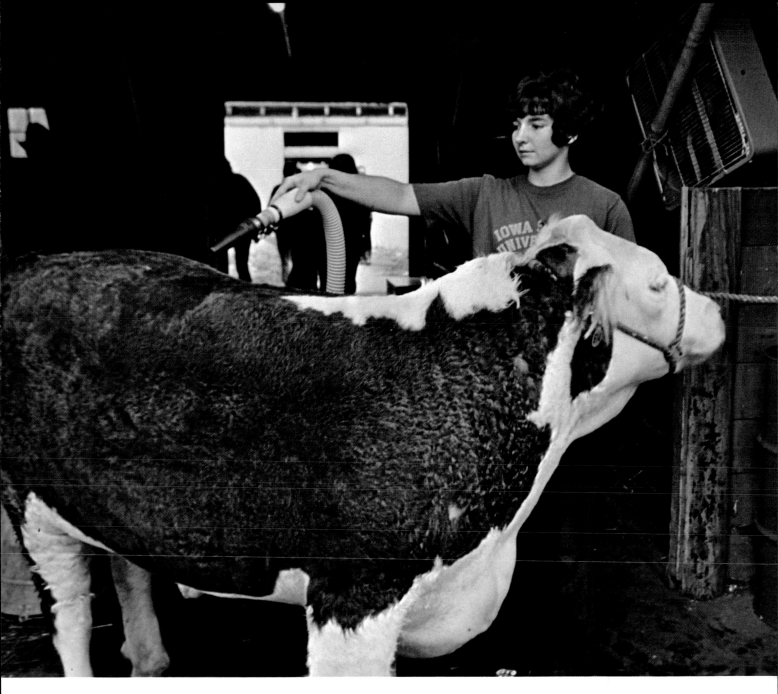

Many of the girls who enter livestock in the Waterloo Cattle Congress spend much time washing, scrubbing, and vacuuming their animals.

IDC photograph.

The annual Midwest Old Settlers' and Threshers' Reunion in Mt. Pleasant started because some Henry County farmers liked to get together with friends and fire up the old steam threshers once a year. Many strangers would come by, and Ray Ernst and his friends decided they might as well put on a "real" show. The result was the first reunion in 1950 — with 12 steam traction engines, 8 old separators, and 2 days of rain. Now there are more than 65 steam engines chugging away during a five-day show that covers all aspects of the pioneer heritage, and, open all summer, a museum, a Midwest Village Main Street, and other elements. During the Labor Day weekend the Reunion takes place. Everything is authenic, including the buildings which were once part of thriving Iowa towns.

IDC photograph.

Photograph by John W. Johnson.

IDC photograph.

Highlight of the year in southwest Iowa is the annual five-day Sidney Rodeo, which attracts the finest bronc and Brahma bull riders on the national competitive tour. The Rodeo's professional troup performs at the Tri-State Championship Rodeo in Fort Madison as well. These events are in August and September. (IDC photograph.)